Lucas County Reads
Lucas County Educational Service Center
Alternate Learning and Career Center
3939 Wrenwood
Toledo, OH 43623

D1518957

At the
Fire Station

This book is dedicated to the
Webster Groves Fire Department,
Webster Groves, Missouri.

Grateful acknowledgement
is made to
the City of Chicago Fire Department

Design and Art Direction
Lindaanne Donohoe Design

Library of Congress Cataloging-in-Publication Data
Greene, Carol.
At the fire station/Carol Greene.
p. cm.
Summary: Describes what might be found in a firehouse
and what the firefighters do there.
ISBN 1-56766-289-7 (hardcover)
1. Fire stations—Juvenile literature.
[1. Fire stations.] I. Title.
TH9148.G7323   1997   96-712
628.9'25—DC20   CIP
                                                                AC

At the Fire Station

By Carol Greene

Photographs by Phil Martin

The Child's World®

It's a quiet day at the firehouse.

Inside the big doors, the big, red fire trucks wait.

Fffft! Fffft!

A firefighter is checking the air in this truck's tires.

Firefighters keep their trucks clean and ready to go at any time.

The fire chief is in charge of the firehouse.

He drives a special car—the command car.

Click! Look at its lights flash!

Some firehouses
have an
assistant chief too.

Here's the pumper—the engine truck.
It carries the hoses. It pumps water from the
hydrant through the hoses.
The pumper is always the first truck at the fire.

The ladder truck carries ladders and hoses too. Sometimes firefighters need ladders to rescue people or spray water into high places.

Some ladder trucks have a tower. It carries firefighters high into the sky.

Big firehouses have many trucks.
At some fire stations, a tanker carries water
and other equipment to a fire.

A small firehouse might have just one truck—a pumper.

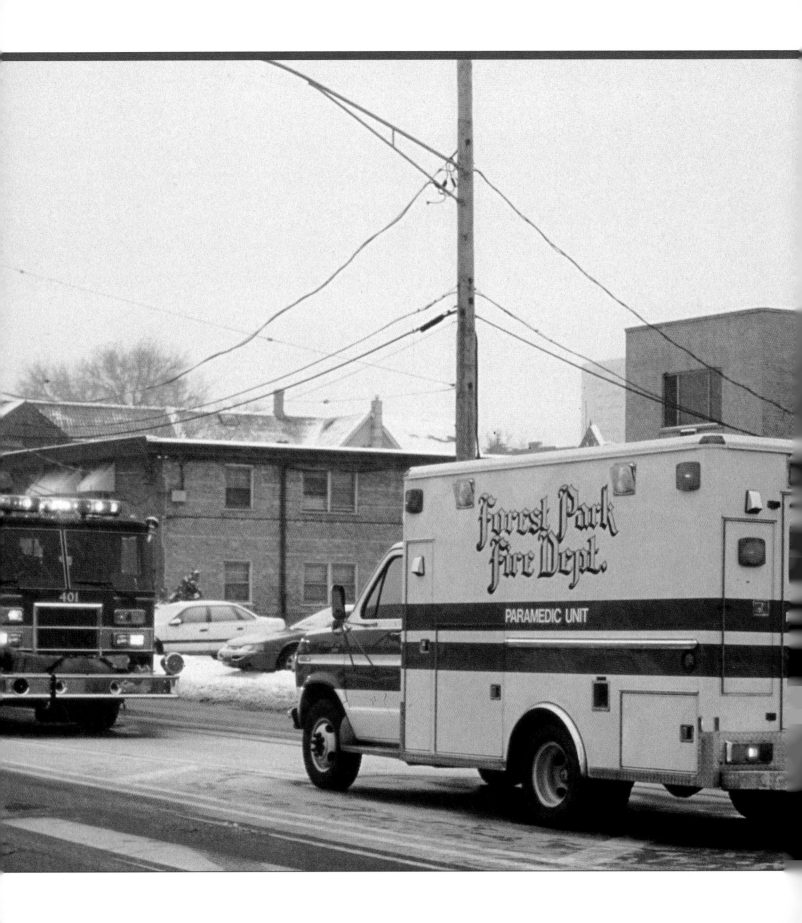

Some firefighters are paramedics too.
They drive the ambulance to help
sick or hurt people.

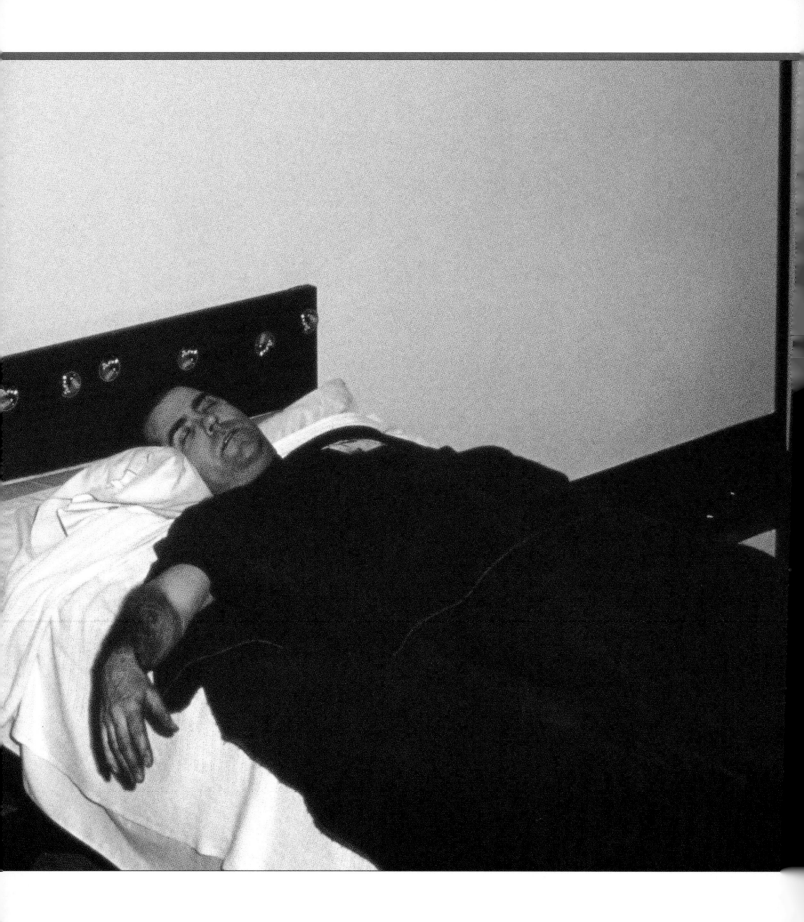

Z Z Z Z Z Z Z Z Z !

Sometimes firefighters work long hours.

They even sleep at the firehouse.

Firefighters often eat meals at the firehouse.
They take turns cooking.

CRASH! THUD! UGH!

Firefighters must stay in good shape.

That's why many firehouses have exercise

equipment.

Sometimes firefighters take classes at the firehouse. They might learn about new equipment or how to talk to people about preventing fires.

Firefighters take good care of their uniforms.
They have special coats, boots, gloves,
and helmets. These must be ready all the time.

Sometimes firefighters wear special masks and carry air tanks. These must be ready too.

This buzzer is a very important alarm.
It tells firefighters when a fire breaks out.
You can hear it all over the firehouse—
and outside the firehouse too.

Some firehouses use a bell instead of a buzzer.

When the buzzer goes off,
firefighters scramble into their clothes.
Then they go to their fire trucks.

Old firehouses
were two stories high.
Firefighters used to slide
down brass poles to get to
the trucks quickly.

Fighting a fire is hard work.

A fire can start at any hour of the day or night.

When they are not fighting a fire or sleeping, firefighters relax.

They might talk or read or just watch TV.

I'm the checkers champ.

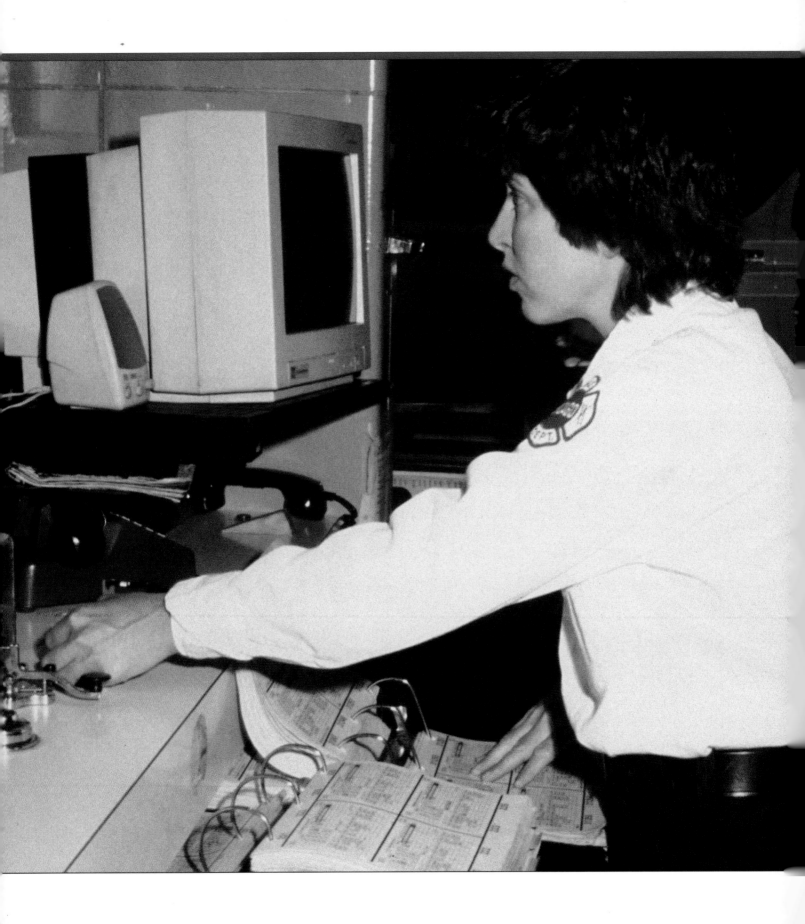

B Z Z Z Z Z Z Z Z Z Z Z !

It's the buzzer!

Hurry, firefighters. Time to go!

It's another fire!

FIRE!   FIRE!

Glossary

hydrant (HY druhnt) — a pipe that draws water for fighting fires

preventing (prih VENT ing) — keeping something from happening

rescue (RES kyoo) — to save from danger

About the Author

Carol Green has written over 200 books for children. She also likes to read books, make teddy bears, work in her garden, and sing. Ms. Green lives in Webster Groves, Missouri.